# You Can Wear Your Heels Now!

A Celebration of Womanhood in Godly Fashion

Erin M. Anderson

# *You Can Wear Your Heels Now!*

A Celebration of Womanhood in Godly Fashion

All scriptures, unless otherwise noted, are taken from the Holy Bible, NKJV and NIV Versions



Published by

On Purpose Publications
Nashville, TN

ISBN 978-0-9827061-0-7

Cover design by Vincent Alexander and PrecisionFX Graphics

Printed in the United States of America

# Dedication

To My Daughter, Rionna—
Girl you were born with heels on. Walk it out!

To My Daughter, Sarah—
God's Fashion Fair Princess.
You Go Girl!

To My Daughter, Gabrielle—
Your Joy Is Mommy's Strength and Victory!

*Thank You*

*You Can Wear Your Heels Now!*

# Contents

*You Can Wear Your Heels Now!*

# Introduction

**A**ny time Jesus speaks, He is calling His people to move forward from where they are. Jesus told Lazarus to "Come forth." He told the damsel to "Arise," and He told the woman to "Go and sin no more." You will never find a place in scripture where Jesus told anyone, "Stay where you are," "go back," or "don't move." He may have told one or two to "be still," but that was only so they could watch God the Father move on their behalf instead of them trying to fix their situation on their own. Even in their stillness, their faith and trust still had to move forward in belief that God was going to come through for them.

God is a God of movement, so naturally, His Son, Jesus, was and is always on the move. Throughout the course of His ministry, He walked and spoke the Word. As He physically walked and talked the Word, He moved right into the destiny and purpose for His life. People's lives were changed because He walked where He was led; and He laid a path of righteousness through the words He spoke for the people He met to walk. His words became the life needed for people to rise up from their personal places of immobility to walk in true purpose and fulfillment. As it was for Jesus, it is the same for you. It's time to walk. It's time to move.

***"In the beginning was the Word and the Word was with God and the Word was God. He was in the beginning with God. All things were made through Him, and without Him nothing was made that was made," John 1:1-3***

The paths of our lives are made by the words that go before us. The steps we take depend on the light of the Word that is available to show us which direction we ought to go. In the beginning, God said "Let there be light," and a pathway was created for light to appear on the earth. On light's path are destiny and life. Destiny encompasses the plans that God has set for every one of his children, plans to prosper them and give them hope and a future (Jer. 29:11). Life includes an abundant life free from torment and distress, but full of love, joy and peace.

At the moment light was formed, a pathway was also created for darkness. On darkness' path are poverty and death, neither of which are limited to finances or the end of living. Darkness carries with it depression and despair, unhappiness and a lack of fulfillment. You have two different paths to choose from with two very different outcomes. The way to your destiny can only be revealed by the light of the Word of God. His word is a lamp to your feet and a light to your path (Psalm 119:105). As God's word moves by His spirit over dark places in your life, it illuminates the steps to your purpose and prosperity; healing and wholeness; happiness and health. The enemy's job is to lead you off course. Through negative words and circumstances, he creates steps of confusion then beckons you to come away from the path that leads to the abundant life God has promised you. God also promises in Isaiah 42:16 that He will turn the darkness into light before you and make the rough places smooth. Your job is to let God's light shine in you so you will know which steps are of the Lord's path and which are of the enemy. How do you do that? You start by opening yourself up to receive from the Spirit of the Lord. Let Him be your teacher and your guide. Let Him show you the way, and the truth and the life. Remember, His word is a lamp to your feet. It will show you the way.

This book is designed to be oil for your lamp, a continuous stream of light pouring on the Word through laughter and love to help your heart and mind comprehend where God has destined your feet to go. It is time for you to walk in your purpose. It's time for you to move. Move from where you are. Move from where you have been. Take off your shoes. Now, take a seat. Take a load off your feet and your mind. It's time to sit at the feet of Jesus and let Him tell you mysteries about you.

There is so much we still don't know about who we are. I bet you didn't know that your feet frighten the enemy beyond measure. Every time he sees this body part, it causes him to shake and tremble like never before. When God cursed the serpent in the garden He told him, "I will put enmity between you and the woman, between your seed and her Seed. He shall bruise your head and you shall bruise His heel" (Gen. 3:15). Since the enemy was cursed to the ground, he is forever postured to watch the people of God walk in their destiny. And he takes advantage of this position to torment and antagonize us through various devices. He bruises our heels through affliction, disappointment, setbacks and trouble. Sometimes we manage to side step him. Other times we stop walking altogether. The light of the Word gives us clear instructions on what to do with the enemy—trample him under foot!

When Jesus began walking in His God given authority, He caused the heavenly and earthly realms to shake under the weight of His steps. He was God walking in the natural covering of the flesh, but He was more importantly man walking under the supernatural covering of the Spirit of God. God the Father, in His infinite wisdom, knew that the fleshly foot of Jesus would be no match for heaven's spiritual enemy. The only way the Seed would be in position to bruise the head of the enemy would be to stand in the authority of God and allow the weight of His glory to crush the serpent under the feet of the anointing. His spiritual covering empowered Him to do above and beyond what his natural flesh could do. When John the Baptist told the ruler of the land "there stands One among you whom you do not know. . .whose sandal strap I am not worthy to loose (or untie)" (Johns 1:26-27), he was putting the spiritual rulers of this age on notice. He knew the power of the feet that would walk after him and recognized the glory of the Mighty Ruler down to the shoes that covered his feet. For His shoes to be untied by man would suggest that flesh has the ability to undo what God has purposed in the earth. John the Baptist knew from personal experience that God had a greater plan for His people than realized. As Christ's forerunner, he knew prophetically that the natural shoes on Jesus' feet symbolized the spiritual covering he was walking in, and under the burden of the gravity of the God's calling on His life, Jesus and all who chose to live in and through God would have the ultimate power to deliver an eternal blow to the enemy's head through their walk.

Women and the enemy have been at war since the days in the garden. God told the enemy that he would put enmity, an everlasting hostility, between his and her seed. I believe God put that antagonism there to keep women on their toes and ready to move to higher places in the Spirit at the sight of the enemy. The enemy forgot that he was messing with God's daughter, fashioned and made by His hands. God never planned to leave her defeated. His plan, called Jesus, redeemed all mankind, including women, to the power and authority they had been designed to walk in. Women around the world are being clothed in a new garment called righteousness as they accept Jesus as their spiritual covering. With this new garment comes new authority that no man or demon can take away from her. All the redeemed woman has to do is wipe the dust of defeat off her feet and slip her feet into the authority of her Heavenly Father and walk out the abundant life!

It's time to celebrate, woman of God. There is a party going on in heaven. The time has come for you to step into your divine purpose. You have waited long enough. The angels already got the party started. They're shouting, singing and blowing their horns. God has rolled out the royal carpet and Jesus is waiting for you to come to the greatest party of your life. Hurry up girl, get your shoes on. Don't be late. You have a date with destiny!

After this revelation you will never look at your shoes the same way again. You have been given POWER!

# Chapter 1

## Woman, Be Heeled

I believe the true test of womanhood is not being able to carry and birth babies or becoming the CEO of a Fortune 500 company. It's the ability to wear high heeled shoes without falling! I am amazed by women who can walk in heels. I have found myself, in the past, and sometimes the present asking myself, "How *do* they do that?" There are no grimaces on their faces as they walk, their backs are straight and they don't flap like birds for balance as they move. I am the most amazed by the woman that can walk in the skinny four inch heels. She seems to glide with ease, like she was born with stilettos on. If you take the time to really think about it, there is much to be said about a woman in heels.

Of course I don't really think wearing heels is *that* serious, but think about it: short women wear heels to make them taller, business women wear heels to make them appear more powerful, and prostitutes wear them to get the onlookers to stop at their corner instead of the corner down the street. High heel shoes are a universal symbol for womanhood around the world, and the ability to wear them ought to be commended.

High heeled shoes have a very unique design. They are slender and delicate, strategically made to raise a woman's heel two, three and sometimes four inches off the ground. To walk in them, a woman must have great balance, strong ankles and a strong back. Her toes must be conditioned to squeeze into a tight space while pressure from the weight of her entire body is on them.

And the arch of support in the center of her foot must be able to bend and bow with the shape of the shoes she is wearing. It takes skills, both physically and mentally, to have the grace to walk in these shoes. And the best part is that the Maker already knew you could wear them and walk it out.

## *Fashioned by Design*

I believe God placed the design of the high heel in the womb of a designer to give women a picture of His ultimate design for their lives. Like the high heeled shoe, God has called women to walk in higher places in the Spirit, elevated and far above the ground of the flesh. We are called to be high and lifted up out of the dust of our mood swings, low self esteem, passivity, and issues. He wants to lift us to a place of confidence in Him and within ourselves that cannot be touched by the enemy. He wants us to walk in strength and purpose, knowing who we are in Him and the power He has given us to carry the weight of the anointing, stand in times of trouble even when the pain is great, and walk upright with assurance in where we are going. All in all, God wants to take us higher in our knowledge of Him, higher in our understanding of who He created us to be, and higher in our relationships with others. And as He takes us higher, He also desires to heighten our sensitivity to the enemy's tactics of deception that are designed to trip us up and cause us to fall.

Genesis 3:15 tells us that God told the serpent in the garden that He would put enmity between him and the woman and between his seed and her Seed. He informed the serpent that the woman's Seed would bruise his head and that his seed would bruise the heel of her seed. "Her Seed" refers to the seed of Christ that lives inside each and every believer. It also refers to all the things that Christ has plans to birth through you into the earth realm—gifts, talents, family, business, ministry and more, not to exclude love, joy, peace, gentleness, meekness, temperance and self control. The seed of Christ encompasses the totality of the calling on your life, and the enemy's greatest desire is to hinder you from fulfilling it. The enemy's seeds are the weapons that he uses to keep you from walking in your purpose—confusion, lies, fear, mistrust, deceit, anger, just to name a few. But keep in mind that his attacks have only been given authority to nip at the heels of your destiny. He tries to deceive you by trying to make you believe that his position to bruise your heels can hinder you from walking, but it can't. Only you can hinder yourself when you refuse to stand up in the authority you have been given by Christ and His anointing to defeat the enemy. If you step on a sharp object, it doesn't have to stop you from walking. All you have to do is raise your heels up off the floor, and walk on your toes!

According to the Podiatry Channel, the human foot combines mechanical complexity and structural strength. The ankle serves as foundation, shock absorber, and propulsion engine. The foot can sustain enormous pressure (several tons over the course of a one-mile run) and provides flexibility and resiliency. The function of the toes, especially the big toe, is to help us balance and to propel us forward during walking or running. The toes, like women, can sustain a tremendous amount of pressure, but they are designed to help the Body move forward. God fashioned us with a unique design in mind, but we have to know our purpose to fulfill God's plan, not just for us, but for the Kingdom of God.

The Word says there will be "enmity" between the woman and the serpent. The word enmity describes an intense hatred or hostility. It doesn't say there might be or there may be enmity. It says there *will* be. That means that you and the enemy are destined to have some battles. The greatness you attempt to produce in your life will experience opposition from the one who doesn't want to see it happen. At this point, you ought to hate the fact that you are still dealing with the same old issues. You should loathe the fact that seeds of mistrust and bitterness have been planted between you and the people closest to you in your life. Those negative seeds are robbing you from experiencing the gifts of love and joy the loved ones in your life are designed to give you. You should detest the fact that things in your life are not lining up with the promises of God, you haven't accomplished what you thought you would. If you are not there yet, my prayer is that you get there fast!

Jesus came to empower us. This empowerment is authorization for us to move toward the "life more abundantly" that God promises us in His word. When we choose to get wrapped up in the enemy's devices and negative words, we stop "growing forward." Instead of advancing from glory to glory to glory, we find ourselves backsliding into a state of defeat and retreat. Fear and low self esteem set in, confusion and doubt begin to drown our hopes and dreams and instead of walking forward, we begin to stand in one place. The spirit of depression and hopelessness cause our knees to buckles and before we know it, our stand has turned to a sit and we are no longer moving or positioned to move at all—forward or backward. Our growth becomes stunted and God's hands become tied, unable to produce in our lives.

Your abundant life is worth fighting for. To all the women out there with bruised heels, bruised emotions, bruised perceptions, and bruised self esteem, it's time to be healed so you can put your Spiritual heels on and start standing. Don't listen to the enemy. You can wear your heels now! Don't listen to yourself. You *have* to wear your heels now-- your life and the lives of your legacy depend on it. Be healed I say, or better yet, Woman, Be Heeled!

### *Kick Off Your Shoes*

*Take a look at where you are in your life as it relates to your dreams, your goals and your relationship to God. Are you sitting waiting for someone else to come stir the waters for you and put you in the pool? Are you standing paralyzed in confusion, not knowing which way to go? Are you walking but still not quite sure if you are going in the right direction? Are there areas where you need healing that are hindering you from moving? Talk to God, your Designer, about it.*

# Chapter 2

## What Not to Wear

One day out of the blue, I decided to clean out my closet. I sat in the middle of the closet floor sifting through storage containers of shoes, old clothes and other items I had packed away. It was amazing how my lack of fashion sense seemed to blare out at me all of a sudden like a fire alarm. After looking through some of the articles, I determined that I was a prime candidate for the television show "What Not to Wear."

---

I had some of the ugliest old shirts, too big pants, too small tops and a lot of shoes that I had worn maybe once or twice. Many of them were heels that hurt my feet the first time I wore them so I never bothered to put them back on. I preferred the comfort of a pair of black leather shoes that I managed to wear most of the time. I had clothes I wore in high school, which I had graduated from many, many years before; things my grandmother had found at yard sales; and accessories that really didn't do much for me. My wardrobe was void of color and lacked character and personality. The fashion police should have given me a ticket a long time ago.

I don't know if you have seen the show "What Not to Wear", but on it unsuspecting people get ambushed by two fashion savvy show hosts whose intentions are to show the ambushees just how bad they dress and to help make them over. They take these people through the truth process of how they look to others by videotaping them at home, work, and other unsuspecting places while criticizing their entire wardrobe from hat to shoe and everything in between. They force the people to stand in front of a three way mirror, so they can see just how bad they look from all sides. They critique their sense of style, or lack thereof, and attempt to break them down to the point of accepting that they need some major help in the "What to Wear" department.

After showing them what a hopeless fashion case they are, the hosts of the show proceed to throw away most, if not all, of the participants' wardrobes. Most people have sentimental attachment to certain articles of clothing in their closet—a favorite ugly shirt or favorite pair of too tight jeans with holes in them. It's normally the shirt that they wore to the concert on their first date with the love of their life who did them wrong. Or a pair of jeans that got them the most attention when they walked through a crowd. The participants would argue and cry, beg and plead not to have that thing they hold so dear thrown away. People's souls become tied to these articles and the only way to introduce a new wardrobe is to untie the emotional attachment keeping them from experiencing freedom from the old self.

The hosts ultimate goals are to show people that they are younger, more alive, and more beautiful than they portray themselves, and then to teach them how to accentuate their bodies to present the best them possible. While on the surface, the Hosts are after the outward appearances of people, an amazing transformation of confidence begins to emerge on the insides of each one as they go through the process of change.

### *New Wardrobe Please*

After you accept Jesus into your life, He and the Holy Spirit become like the hosts on What Not to Wear. They never criticize, but they do begin to take the Word of God and show you yourself—the good, the bad and the ugly. Truth is never fun to look at. For so long we have walked around doing and being the best we know how to be thinking that we're fine, but it's not until we give the Lord permission to get into our closet, do we see the truth about the mess that lies inside of our hearts. After He begins to rummage around and show us what is really there, even though it hurts to hear it, He keeps telling us the truth until we come to accept that the fashion fair on the inside of us is merely a parade of rags that need to be exchanged for riches.

We all have a hard time letting go of the past, regardless of whether our experiences were good or bad. Our personalities and identities are shaped by our experiences. What we often don't realize is that we drag our past experiences into our present situations, ultimately affecting our future circumstances and relationships. Our now perceptions are shaped by our past. Even if the past was great, the future can be greater if you will make room for the new experiences.

There is a fear in letting go of what we know and what we have experienced because our knowledge is a security blanket to our lives. If what we know is a great past experience, it's hard to believe there is the possibility of a greater one, so we are scared to let go fearing that we will never have great again. If what we know is not so great, the fear of the negative experience reoccurring becomes so great that we do everything we can to shield and protect ourselves from ever experiencing it again. When we put up walls or refuse to let go, we also block God's ability to show us the greater love and life he has for us. It's hard to believe that you can ever love more than you did then, but you can. It's even harder to believe that you will find love where you found abuse then, but you will. You have to trust what the Hosts tell you and be willing to take a risk. Truthfully, what do you really have to lose?

To many people on the What Not to Wear show, having someone come in and throw all of their personal things away is just like having someone come in and throw their identity away. They often try to reason and justify why they bought an ugly t-shirt or why they still have, and wear, leg warmers from the flash dance era. These things have become part of their identity, and as the hosts continue working with them, it becomes apparent that the bigger issue is that the things people wear more often represent how they really feel about themselves. Many of the people being stripped of their things are distraught because they feel like they are being stripped of themselves, not to mention they really like their things. Think about it-- after being stripped of everything you know, all you are left with is a choice—choose to remain void of identity or choose to trust the hosts to identify a look that suits you and transform you into a new person. So, what are *you* wearing?

I asked myself that same question while I sat in my closet. The more I thought about it, I began to realize that I wore the same pair of flat black shoes almost every day. Sometimes I would even change my clothes just so I could wear those shoes. I didn't care that they weren't very fashionable. And truthfully, there really wasn't anything very special about them other than they were comfortable. They weren't the cutest pair of shoes—they were sort of square toe and boot looking, almost like a man's dress shoe, but they were made out of very soft leather. Because of the size and shape of my feet I was actually excited when I bought them to finally find a casual shoe that didn't make my feet scream. They really weren't shoes to shout about, but I liked them. Most importantly, me feet liked them.

If I were on the show, I know my black shoes would be the first thing they would try to make me throw away. The shoes hindered every ounce of creativity in my wardrobe, but they were so comfortable. Get concerned when the events of your life become too comfortable and you find yourself doing the same thing the same way, everyday. When life begins to have a religious pattern of behaviors—wake, work, home, sleep; wake, work, home, sleep—day after day after day, ask God to breathe new life in you. When you find yourself stagnant, not progressing in your personal, social, or spiritual relationships, ask God to show you what is hindering you from living a life where every day is a new challenge, a new adventure, and a new glory. If the soles of your shoes are worn in the same area because you walk the same mental and emotional path every day, it's time to go shopping for a new pair. The Lord of Hosts has come today to ambush your spiritual life and show you what needs to be removed from your closet. He wants to fill it and you with some new things.

## Kick Off Your Shoes

*What are some things that God wants to throw out of your closest? Is it your attitude? Is it the way you think about yourself? Is it the way you treat others? Take a few moments to go through your internal closet. Are there any areas that need to be purged to make room for the new garments God wants to give you? Talk to God, your Designer, about it.*

# Chapter 3

## Momma Needs a New Pair of Shoes

**T**he craziest thing is that I didn't even realize what I was doing before I did it. I was standing in the middle of the room talking to some of the girls at church and the next thing I knew, I was slipping my feet out of my flat black leather shoes. I walked around the room in just my socks for a while, saying hello to a few other people who had come out that night for bible study. I'm sure some of them were wondering why

I didn't have any shoes on. Eventually, we all started moving towards the door to leave. And there sat my black shoes in the middle of the floor--empty. A friend of mine picked them up and handed them to me and the next thing I knew, I was asking my pastor to witness me tossing my comfortable, wear with everything even if they don't really match, did I say comfortable, shoes in the garbage can. And then I walked out the door.

When God begins to press on your heart areas about you that need to change, He does it in the most gentle and loving way. God had been talking to me for months about His desire to change the path my feet were walking. I walked in such low self esteem and compromise that I was undermining the greatness of God inside me. The path your life takes is determined by the thoughts you think about yourself and those around you. Proverbs 23:7 says, "As a man thinks in his heart, so is he." I can remember sitting in service and having an overwhelming sense that God wanted me to walk differently and think differently about myself. All I kept hearing Him say to me throughout the night was "take off your shoes."

That night reminded me of Moses on the mountain with the burning bush (see Exodus 3). The bush got his attention, sort of like the detriment of my wardrobe and my shoes got mine. When Moses turned to see why the bush that was on fire was not burning up, God asked him to remove his shoes because where he was standing was holy ground. Once Moses recognized the presence of God and acted on the instructions to remove his shoes, God introduced Himself to Moses in a way He never had before and shared the purpose and plans that He had for Moses to be the deliverer of God's chosen people.

***"Moreover he said, I am the God of thy father, the God of Abraham, the God of Isaac, and the God of Jacob. And Moses hid his face; for he was afraid to look upon God. "Exodus 3:6***

God revealed Himself to Moses in a way that Moses had never encountered before. He gave him instructions, made promises of victory, commissioned him and empowered him with the power needed to succeed in all the things he was being asked to do. Despite God's presence and promises, Moses had a hard time receiving the new path for his life because "he was afraid to look upon God." Moses had so many negative thoughts about himself and his ability to do the things God wanted him to do, that for every great thing God told him he wanted to do through him, Moses had a rebuttal.

***"But Moses said to God, Who am I that I should go to Pharaoh, and that I should bring the children of Israel out of Egypt?" Exodus 3:11***

***"And Moses answered and said, But, suppose they will not believe me, nor listen to my voice, suppose they say, The Lord has not appeared to you.'" Exodus 4:1***

***"And Moses said unto the lord, O my Lord, I am not eloquent, neither before not since you have spoken to your servant; but I am slow of speech and slow of tongue." Exodus 4:10***

Moses' needed to take a trip to the three way mirror to see all of the angles of his thoughts that were hindering him from walking in his destiny. Sometimes we are so afraid of being inadequate that we hesitate in taking our shoes off to see what the Lord wants to show us about ourselves. God had great things to show Moses. I had been seeking God for a new experience with Him, and I wanted to see more about the calling on my life, but little did I know that taking off my shoes would be such a life changing experience.

### *Deep Down in My "Sole"*

I still can't believe I threw my shoes away. I mean, tossing them in the trash made not wearing them again a permanent thing. There was nothing I could do to get those shoes back, which is probably why the Holy Spirit prompted me to throw them away, not just agree to not wear them again. He knew the temptation to put them back on would be too great. Radical change in thought patterns calls for radical measures. I had reached a point in my life where I had become too comfortable. Things had stopped moving and I had stopped reaching and believing for more from God. I had become complacent and content with the mediocrity of my life, but God was and still is determined to get more out of me. There is greatness inside me and you and we can't be afraid to reach for it.

When I was younger, tennis shoes were my thing. I would venture to say that I was more *like* the tennis shoes than I liked to wear the tennis shoes. I was very supportive to people around me, but I was laced up pretty tight. It was very hard to get into me. I didn't trust people enough to let them in. I liked people and wanted them to like me, so most of the time I let people run all over me instead of standing up for myself. I would do anything to help people, to support them when they needed a friend, but I didn't let them get too close to me because I thought they would hurt me. It was very hard for people to tell that they had hurt me because of my thick "sole." I didn't like conflict, so I just took whatever was done to me without saying a word.

I remember how I treated my tennis shoes after a basketball game. I wouldn't bother untying them before pulling them off. I would throw them into the closet until the next game, never caring enough about them to set them on the shoe rack. They were my basketball shoes, and I only wore them to play basketball. Unfortunately I felt people only wore me when they needed me for something, never truly caring enough about me to untie me to see what I was really all about. What is even sadder is that I saw myself exactly how they treated me. They were merely a mirror to the madness in my mind about how I felt about myself. People will only do to you what you allow. Most of the time you will let them do to what you normally do to yourself.

By now you should be able to tell that I had some real soul issues. The shoes you wear in the natural have no bearing on your destiny. But the shoes you wear can serve as symbolic of the spiritual and emotional battle going on with your personal walk with the Lord. The wrong mindset about you can cause degrees of pain and discomfort in your life and within relationships that are unnecessary. I was most comfortable with myself when I wore tennis shoes because they allowed me to hide. They helped to mask my self-conscious areas, like my big feet and my personal insecurities. They gave me reason to wear big baggy jeans and sweatshirts, so I wouldn't have to endure the comments about me being skinny. I could wear my hair pulled back in one ponytail, instead of wearing it down in curls, because curls were too dressy for jeans and tennis shoes. It didn't take too much effort to brush the hair back and put on the ponytail holder. Sometimes I didn't even brush it. I just pulled it back. Do you see where I am going with this? I felt very relaxed and protected, particularly from cold air and criticism when I wore my tennis shoes. They gave me the excuse to be lazy, the excuse not to put forth any effort, and the excuse to hide myself. I played sports so most people didn't even challenge me about what I had on. It was ok for me to be rough and tough looking, in jogging pants and wind suits, as opposed to dresses and makeup. It was ok to be hard and not show emotion. At least that is what I thought. I walked around even then like everything was alright, but I hated who I was. I realized that there was a lady underneath, but she had been covered up and comfortable so long, she was afraid to come out. It took almost ten years for me to decide it was time to come out of my messed up self because I was afraid to be the real me. Please don't let it take you that long. Now is the time to move.

I still can't believe the Lord got me out of those shoes and those thoughts about myself. And I'm telling you, to get me out of those shoes it could only have been the Lord with a greater plan for my feet than the limitations they put on my "self" expression. There is a danger in wearing one particular pair of shoes all the time. You always end up going the same places. All of the other shoes get neglected and your feet don't know what to do in any other shoes. I do have other shoes—dress shoes, tennis shoes, sandals, and heels—but I loved those black shoes. They were always the first pair I thought about when it was time to put on shoes. I put them on to go out to the mail box; I put them on to go to work; I even managed to put them on to go to church. Truthfully, I didn't even realize just how comfortable I had become until I got called out by my pastor about my shoes.

One day, my pastor smiled at me as she greeted me after service. "I'm liking that outfit," she said, making reference to a flower print black and white jacket and black pants. "Except for those shoes. We are going to have to do something about those shoes." No one had ever challenged me about my shoes before. And of course my response was "But, I like these shoes. What's wrong with these shoes?" My feelings were so hurt. How could she not like my shoes? She didn't know how comfortable they were. And well, how comfortable they were! "Why don't you try some heels," she said. "That outfit would be really nice if you had on some heels."

It's funny how we get challenged in the small areas of ourselves and it makes us feel like our very existence is being challenged. Prophetically that is exactly what was happening. It is absolutely necessary to explain to you that my pastor has been gifted by God to challenge people in areas of the heart and mind that hinders them from being everything God has called them to be. She is the queen of heels and fashion, but she is also a woman that stays open to God's challenge to be the best person she can be. She preaches, prays, and dances in heels, but she is willing to sacrifice the self she is comfortable with to become the woman God has called her to be regardless of what others think—now that's heel walking!

Prophetess Lorelle S. Rich has been my mentor for more than twelve years. I have watched her walk with God as a single woman, a married woman, a mother and now a pastor; and her spiritual fruit and confidence in Christ far exceeds her external self. For Prophetess Rich to tell me to "try some heels," knowing the spiritual dimensions she walks in and the kinds of heels she wears, she might as well have been asking me to walk on water.

## Kick Off Your Shoes

*What thoughts do you have about yourself that hinder your confidence in Christ? Talk to God, your Designer, about it.*

# Chapter 4

## Walk on Water

**T**he night I threw my shoes away, rain on the street soaked my socks as I walked through the parking lot to my car. As I sat in my car wondering what I had done, the Lord whispered to me, "It's time to walk on the water." I laughed as I drove home in soggy socks, thinking "I wonder what kind of shoes God is going to ask me to walk in tomorrow?" Little did I know the real "heeling" experience He had in store for me.

***"But the boat was now in the middle of the sea, tossed by the waves, for the wind was contrary. Now in the fourth watch of the night Jesus went to them, walking on the sea. And when the disciples saw Him walking on the sea, they were troubled, saying, "It is a ghost!" And they cried out for fear. But immediately Jesus spoke to them, saying, "Be of good cheer! It is I; do not be afraid." And Peter answered Him and said, "Lord, if it is You, command me to come to You on the water." So He said, "Come." And when Peter had come down out of the boat, he walked on the water to go to Jesus." Matthew 14:24-29***

## *So, Get Out of the Boat*

Peter had a "take your shoes off" experience that day in the boat when he saw Jesus on the water in the middle of a storm. Jesus didn't actually say, "Take off your shoes" and he didn't tell him the water he was standing on was Holy water either. But think about it. Only holiness could ask you to get out of a place of comfort like your little boat called *self*, knowing that you are deathly afraid of drowning in failure, and call you to walk forward to meet Him in an ocean of possibilities farther than you can even imagine. Oceans have swallowed up things far larger than you or me, like the Titanic, but Peter was being given the chance do the impossible if he was willing to trust and walk it out.

Anytime God asks you to step out of something, He is preparing you to step into something new. Most of the time, the "something" God is calling you to step out of is yourself—your mind, will, and emotions. You have to be willing to risk everything about you—what you think, what you know, and what you think you know in order to experience new life. What you like, what you prefer, and what you think you want is irrelevant. The parts of your personality that you have come to believe are "just the way you are" or the thoughts you think about yourself that you just can't let go of really do have to go. The only way to step into something new is to walk out of the fear of losing the old.

God knows what's best for you. He knows the thoughts and plans He has for you, plans to prosper you and not harm you, to give you hope and a future (Jer. 29:11). He desires that you know His plans, too. Why wouldn't you want to get out of your boat? You know as well as I do that your boat has a few cracks and leaks. Water seeps in every now and then making you feel like you are drowning. Everything is fine when the seas around you are calm and allowing you to control the direction of your boat; but let a major storm hit your life. The only reason you haven't sunk by now is because of the lifeguard called the Lord who has always been there looking to save you when you needed rescuing. He reaches down in the middle of every storm just before the waters swallow you up, drags you back to shore, and pumps the water out of your lungs while breathing in new life. Then you have to start over on the journey. He has done it time and time again. Don't you think it's time to make it through to the other side?

All of us seem to believe that we are the captains of our lives. The truth is that God knows the course we must sail to get where he has destined for us to land. Without his guidance, our ships are destined to wreck. We have two choices—get out of our boats and walk on the water or get out of our boats and let God build us a new one. Either way it's time to do something new and different. The old thing is not getting us anywhere any faster. After your last experience, I can' t blame you for not wanting to get back in the water. But in order to get to the other side, you have to cross over the waters again. Life has thrown me a lot of storms, but I refuse to be carried away. I want to be and achieve everything God has for me, even if it requires some crazy action on my part.

## *The Crazy Factor*

Many people are hindered from moving forward in life because there is usually a "crazy factor" involved in stepping out of what is familiar into the unknown with the Lord. You may desire to change careers, to start a business, to leave that old crazy boyfriend because you know he is not God's best for you, but you are overly concerned about what other people are going to think. The first someone that will think you are crazy will probably be you. Most of the time, we are our greatest hindrances to having better lives. We don't think we deserve it. We don't feel that we are worthy and we think our inadequacies are larger than the power within us. When we step out and do something that we have never done before, we usually feel crazy for trying. I'm sure you have asked yourself these questions before:

"What are you doing?"

"You know you don't know how to do that?"

"What makes you think they will pick you?"

"You're not even qualified for that job?"

"Whose going to listen to what you have to say?"

"You're no expert."

Moses took off his shoes in obedience to a talking bush on fire. You cannot tell me he didn't feel crazy. I'm sure he wondered what people would think if they saw him, and probably even looked over his shoulder every now and then to make sure no one was watching. But because he recognized God's Spirit in what seemed crazy, he was willing to risk his image to listen and obey. At the heart of Moses' stepping out he received instructions concerning his purpose. He experienced God in ways that he had never done before and they built a wonderful relationship in the process. His life was transformed all because he was willing to separate himself from the shoes he was walking in and put his feet on the ground of the new direction awaiting him. A new path of life was created for him and for a nation of people who needed a new life too.

There is a danger in getting too comfortable on a certain path, or in a certain pair of shoes. You begin to set limitations around yourself (and your wardrobe!) if you are not willing to take off the old shoes and put on the new ones God has fashioned and designed new direction just for your feet.

***"Therefore, if anyone is in Christ, he is a new creation; old things are passed away; behold all things have become new." 2 Corinthians 5:17***

Once we give our lives to Christ, our feet are supposed to walk in new directions. All of our old steps are supposed to change—our attitudes, our old ways of doing things, our old emotions, our old response, even our old ways of looking at ourselves, are all suppose to move in a new direction. The old must come off so the glorious love of Christ can rise up in us and help us walk the path God has set for us.

To walk down the road of purpose you have to be strong just like you have to be strong to walk in high heels. You have to have strong ankles, strong knees, strong legs, and a strong back (not to mention great balance) to be able to stand in those shoes. Women are not born knowing how to walk in high heels, just like we are not born knowing how to be strong in the Lord according to his purpose for us. But He is here on the waters to help us. He is asking us to come. It only takes one step.

## Kick Off Your Shoes

Pray this Prayer:

*Lord,*

*Thank you for helping me take off the old me. I want to walk in a new way. I give my old shoes to you--my old thoughts, old habits, and old emotions that have caused me to walk away from my purpose in you. Adorn my feet with your shoes of peace so I can walk according to your purpose for my life. In Jesus Name, Amen.*

*Now, talk to God, your Designer, about where your feet are destined to go next.*

# Chapter 5

# Bunions, Blisters, and Broken Heels

**Y**ou better believe I was very intimidated about trading my tennis shoes and flat black casuals for a pair of high heeled shoes. The prophetic push from my pastor to "try some heels" just wouldn't go away. I knew that there was more to it than prancing around in a new pair of shoes looking cute. I was in training for the greater life God wanted me to have and experience. After trying to walk in my new self and new shoes for a few days, I was ready to declare that my feet were not made for heels. In order to make the abstract spiritual change more real to my everyday life, I picked a pair of high heeled shoes and chose to walk in them for a number of days. I spent the majority of my life in the comfort of spacious tennis shoes, with a tremendous amount of support for the arch and the ankles. Training my entire body, not just my feet, to walk in heels was a greater task than I could ever imagine.

The heels at first were extremely tight and they pinched my toes together at the end. My feet are long and narrow (a whopping size 11) so heels to me make my feet look even longer and narrower. Everything that was wrong with me before seemed to magnify. I have bunion bones on the sides of my feet that are sensitive to pressure, so the squeezing of my feet into the small, narrow shoes made my feet scream. My ankles turned when I tried to walk causing me to stumble awkwardly. I had no idea what I was doing, and I felt foolish.

I am convinced that the greatest pains on earth are the pinky toes of a woman whose feet have been rubbed raw by her new shoes! Talk about torture! Have you ever tried to walk with pain shooting through your foot with every step? If the enemy was smarter he would leave women's heels alone and mess with their toes. Those little digits can bring a person to tears when stepped on, hit, or rubbed raw by a pair of high heeled shoes! I have never felt any pain like it in my life. I had just started making myself wear heels more often. The heels had become my natural reminder that I was in supernatural training to walk in new dimensions in the Spirit. If I wanted to walk as a new woman in Christ, I had to learn how to walk in my new shoes.

Whether it is in spirit realm or in the natural, you have to practice something new to you in order to become skilled in that thing. If you are learning how to pray, you have to practice prayer. If you are learning how to sew, you have to practice sewing. You can never be perfected in an area that you aren't willing to practice. If you really want to learn how to walk as a new woman in Christ, you have to practice what you desire. You have to practice more love, more peace, more joy and more forgiveness. You have to practice reaching out to others, asking for help, and submitting. Remember practice makes perfect, but that doesn't mean that you will ever be perfect in those areas. What it does mean is that Christ will become perfected in your life and He will give you the supernatural ability to do all things.

The more I walked, the more comfortable I became. Always be concerned where comfort lies. When we start to get comfortable we sometimes get a little too confident in our own abilities. I started wearing my heels to work and to church for prayer and I felt good about it. I was proud of myself, and just when I thought I was pretty confident in my ability to walk, I got small blisters on my baby toes and you would have thought my entire foot was being eaten by wolves. In the midst of me trying to prove to myself that I could do it, my feet screamed in agony as I took steps, until I had to stop and place band-aids over the areas that were worn. Even after the band-aids, I still felt like crying. I couldn't wait to get home to pull those shoes off. If the truth be told, I felt like throwing my heels away, too.

God used those blisters as a friendly reminder that I need Him to walk out my destiny, and no matter how much He elevates me, it will always be because of His ability, not mine. Isn't it just like God to show us that we don't have the ability to do anything without him.

You better know it did not take me long to go out and buy another pair of comfortable black shoes. I realized that I wasn't quite ready for the heels. There were still some areas of pride and inferior thinking that had to be purged out before I could really walk in the truth of God. This time I bought a pair of boot like shoes that had more of a heel than the last pair I threw away. They were still black and comfortable but the heel was about a two inch high wide rubber heel with plenty of ground coverage to keep me from falling. In the Spirit they were more like combat boots, which is exactly what I needed on my feet to fight the good fight of faith that was necessary for me to arrive to my personal place of destiny. I wanted to be a woman whose confidence and trust were in God, and who walked in the power and authority given to her through her relationship with Jesus Christ. I was no longer willing to remain the woman who needed other people to validate her, to encourage her, or to fill her voids.

You can do every natural thing you can think of to walk in new dimensions of yourself; but if your mindset and thought patterns don't change, you will find yourself slipping back into old walking habits. I told you already that I advanced from the tennis shoe mentality to the casual shoe mindset, but the compromising patterns of behavior that were set into how I thought about myself were stronger than a fortified city. Even after I courageously threw my flat black shoes away, and I began to wear my heels, I would do great for a season—thinking confidently, acting confidently, praying confidently, but after a while when things started to get a little dull, or the pains of change started to hurt, I would find my feet slipping back into the comfortable behaviors of the flat black shoe.

### *Broken Heels*

Don't ever give yourself the option of compromise. When you compromise on becoming the woman God has chosen you to be, you end up yielding to the lies of the enemy concerning you. Confidence in the process of change, confidence in the Hosts of change (Jesus and the Holy Spirit), and confidence in your ability to make it to the end requires trust, reliance, boldness and faith. Without these things, you are destined to stay in the low place. Don't settle for less. Even if you have to go back a little, don't stay back. Keep pressing forward. There is no return policy on your destiny. The word of God says that His word can't return to Him void. It must accomplish was He has set for it to do. So no matter how hard you try to run or how many times you try to hide, you cannot escape the plans God has for you.

I tried to run back to my place of comfortability. God even graced me to stay there a little while. But the agitation I experienced all around me caused me to get up again to pursue. I walked that second round of black shoes, but I had to wrestle with the enemy call "Me." I was my own hold up. I was crying out for God to deliver me from myself; but if I wasn't willing to take the shoes off and keep them off, I could never go higher.

I was so determined to get free from me that I allowed God to walk me through the deeply rooted issues of my life until the heel broke on my new black shoes. When you let God heal you, he breaks the yokes of bondage off of your neck so you can turn down a new path. It is brokenness that promotes you in the spirit. God promotes the humble and contrite or crushed in spirit. I knew that I had been delivered when I looked down at my feet, after praying and making the necessary adjustments needed in my thoughts and my character, and saw the rubber sole of my shoe broken. How it happened, I'm not sure. All I know is that I refused to accept defeat. I refused to accept mediocrity. I was determined to stay in God's presence until the old thoughts about me disappeared. This round of deliverance was not comfortable. This round was pure hell. This round made me step into the three way mirror called the Father, Son and Holy Spirit and finally face the facets of my life: the absence of my birth father, and the rejection of another one, verbal abuse and attempted rape, loss of friends, death of loved ones, family secrets and self hatred marked by thoughts of suicide. But the Hosts were with me through it all. The promise never to leave me or forsake me rang true. The miracle working power of God has broken the mental bondages that held my feet in chains. Now it's time to go up higher.

God is going to get the glory out of your life regardless. How long it takes and the process it takes is up to you. I can't tell you it won't hurt. I can't tell you that you won't want to go back. But you can't. You were created to walk in higher dimensions. You have a higher calling on your life and no blisters, bunions, or broken heels can stop you now.

## Kick Off Your Shoes

***Tell the Father, your Designer, all about it. He is here.***

# Chapter 6

## Get Dressed For Favor

**T**here are different shoes for different places our feet must walk in life. We don't usually put much thought into what our foot apparel is saying about us. The types of shoes we have on either tells others what mood we are in, where we have been or where we are going—tennis shoes to the gym, glass slippers to the ball, combat boots to war or flip flops to the beach. The confusion comes in when we wear tennis shoes with a ball gown, or flip flops with a ski jacket, or glass slippers with bed clothes. Someone looking at you will be confused about where you are going, and rightfully so. Others not being able to tell where you are going is not the worst when it comes to you reaching your purpose and destiny. The worst is you not knowing where you are going and not being properly dressed to match the favor that is on your feet.

## *Teach Me What To Wear*

After stripping the participants of their past garments, but before sending them out to buy their new wardrobe, the hosts of the "What Not To Wear" show take time to show the participants fashionable outfits that complement their shape and life. They suggest colors and styles that look better on them than what they had and they show them how to take items in a store and mix and match them to bring out their own personal styles. Most of what they suggested are completely opposite from what the participants are used to wearing. For someone whose wardrobe is mostly black, they suggest lots of color. For women who have lots of sweatpants and jeans, they suggest nice trousers or skirts to complement their feminine form. After the teaching of what to wear takes place, the hosts give the participants each a credit card with a $5000 shopping limit and they send them out to build their new wardrobes.

Knowing that the participants are still not one hundred percent on board with the “becoming new thing”, the hosts set rules about what cannot be bought in the stores, which usually include any items that resemble the things that were previously thrown out of the old wardrobes. We naturally gravitate to what is familiar, so you probably know what most people are drawn to first—the old.

The show hosts always watched from a nearby room to monitor what was being bought for the new wardrobes. They were faithful to come to the rescue of any backsliding participants who started to buy off limit items. Their roles at this point are to keep them pressing to complete their new assignment. Thank God, that just like the hosts of the show, there is a host of angels cheering on your supernatural transformation. We agree to let the Lord change us and rearrange us but the minute it gets hard or we get discouraged, we want to walk back into the familiar old place. Don't look back!

The Word of God gives keys to being dressed for your date with destiny. Esther was an orphan who had never walked in the corridors of a palace before (see the book of Esther). And since she did not know what would give her the favor she needed to be chosen, she yielded to Hegai, one of the king's servants, to be taught and trained. If it had not been for him showing her what to wear, she would have never been dressed to draw favor from the king. She was properly prepared because she allowed herself to stripped of her orphan garments and redressed in royal ones. Esther was willing to humble herself to be taught by an insider to the kingdom. Her destiny was to be Queen, but without the proper dressing of the favor she needed, she would have never been chosen or ready to walk it out.

*Watch What You're Wearing*

The worst outfit to put on when trying to find favor with the Lord is pride. Pride is a garment that causes the Lord to look away from you. It doesn't matter if you have dressed your walk up in the nicest garment you can find. You may walk the walk and talk the talk like you are Miss "I Got This Thing Together", but the pride on you looks like a burlap sack to the Lord.

Pride is a very sneaky demon that can cause destruction as God is working to construct a new you. The minute I began to get confident in my ability to walk in my heels, I stopped asking God to help me. I was so desperate for His help when I was depressed and discouraged about the state of my life, but the minute things started to look up, I stopped asking and depending on Him as much. The most dangerous thing we can do as God builds our confidence and esteem is to think that somehow we had something to do with it. Pride can manifest in many ways—selfishness, self pity, self sufficiency, and even self confidence and self esteem.

When we give self the glory for advancement in our emotions, our character or our giftings, we are robbing God of His glory and that is one thing He will not share with anyone, not even his daughters.

Not all women that wear heels are dressed in the true fashion of the power and authority of God. You have to be very careful not to mistake a person's walk and talk for righteousness if the fruit doesn't line up. There are three sisters that you have to watch out for, and at any time any one of us can become any of them if we're not careful. They have a form of favor but in a mixed up fashion.

The first sister wants to be elevated because she feels powerless on the inside. She wears heels and make up to mask how low she truly feel about herself on the inside and often times she pretends to be confident while depending on other people's acceptance to determine how she measures her worth. This woman's name is Miss "So Low Power" or (Solo) because until she stops waiting on other people or things to lift her up, she will be mistreated, sad and alone. Loneliness will be the garment she lives in and she will never be treated any better than she thinks of herself. Miss So Low has trust issues and expects that people will disappoint and abuse her, so they do. She has trouble believing that people's love for her is genuine, so she goes overboard to be accepted. You would never know that a woman that looks as good as she does could really feel as low about herself as Miss So Low does.

Miss So Low has a sister that acts completely opposite. Unless you look really closely you wouldn't even know they were sisters. This sister prides herself on not being seen as a flat heeled low self esteem woman with no power like her sister. It's all about image for her. She elevates herself to a place where she can look down on others, so people won't have the chance to think low of her. This is why people call her Miss "Power Trip." She brags and boasts of her accolades just so everyone will know that she wears the heels. She manipulates people to get what she wants, both men and women, but she eventually gets tripped up in her own arrogance, because she never considers the people she steps on when she walks. Miss Power Trip pushes people away because of the fear that they will learn that her real esteem is as low as Miss So Low's. Her ego can't handle people thinking she is any less than what she appears to be so she puffs herself up to keep people away.

Of the three fold cord of sisters of women that a woman aiming for destiny should never want to dress like, this last sister is the most dangerous of all. She is sweet and kind, seeming to befriend you to the end. But be careful because she will watch what you wear to get what you have, only to come back with a shoe a half inch higher than yours the next time. She really wants all the power, all the attention, all of the praise and can't stand for others to look or be better than she is. She secretly despises other women that have more than her, achieve greater than her, or get more glory than her. Her accessories are jealousy and envy and because her name is Miss "Power Competition" and she will do whatever is necessary, by any means necessary, to get ahead of you. She will get close enough to you to push past you on purpose just to get the higher position. Her greatest difficulty is celebrating her sisters.

Of the three sisters called So Low, Power Trip, and Power Competition, we all have the potential to become them if we don't allow the Designer to teach us what garments real Godly women wear. The competitive nature that the enemy stirs up among women is the most dangerous dress any of us could put on. Real women wear Godly fashions made of fine fabrics of trust, love, and forgiveness. They are not afraid to let the Lord look at them before they leave the house, to be sure that their attitudes, both about themselves and other women, line up with God's plan for real sisterhood.

There are enemies among us and they are hindering us from trusting one another. They tempt us to backbite, gossip and trip one another up; and if each of us were to open our purses, pull out our compacts and look in the mirror we would see them. It's us! We have become enemies to ourselves and each other because we have not tapped into the truth about the real power and purpose in our womanhood. We have become easy targets for the deceiver's lies and once we have accepted them as truth we begin to relate to one another in conflict.

God does not desire for us to misuse and mistreat each other to get what we want. He wants us to be dressed in the security of His love so we can walk in the authority of His power and assist and encourage each other as we walk out our individual purposes and destinies. Every time we put on a garment of pride, we exchange our heels for other kinds of shoes. This causes us to walk in realms we were never intended. Pride often goes best with flat shoes called inferiority or a low heel called inadequacy. It might even let us wear a mid high heel shoe that gives us the feeling that we have stepped into God's power, but we lack the strength needed to walk out the course. These shoes make us walk in fear which has the ability to make up veer completely off course.

Walking in any shoe other than the high calling God has called you to walk in leads to less than the abundant life that is awaiting you. That's why, no matter what you do, you have to be sure to dress for God's favor and pick the right pair. The choice belongs to you. What are you really waiting for?

### Kick Off Your Shoes

*What kind of sister are you to other women? Are you part of the So Low, Power Trip or Power Competition sisterhood? If so, talk to God, your Designer, about it. Tell him the areas of your character that need to be returned and exchanged for true sisterhood. Destiny awaits and the party is for more than just you.*

# Chapter 7

## Now... Stand

*"Finally, be strong in the Lord and in his mighty power. Put on the full armor of God so that you can take your stand against the devil's schemes. For our struggle is not against flesh and blood, but against the rulers, against the authorities, against the powers of this dark world and against the spiritual forces of evil in the heavenly realms. Therefore put on the full armor of God, so that when the day of evil comes, you may be able to stand your ground, and after you have done everything, to stand. Stand firm then, with the belt of truth buckled around your waist, with the breastplate of righteousness in place, and with your feet fitted with the readiness that comes from the gospel of peace. In addition to all this, take up the shield of faith, with which you can extinguish all the flaming arrows of the evil one. Take the helmet of salvation and the sword of the Spirit, which is the word of God. And pray in the Spirit on all occasions with all kinds of prayers and requests. With this in mind, be alert and always keep on praying for all the saints" Ephesians 6:10-18 (NIV)*

Stand against the devils' schemes

*Don't be deceived*

Stand your ground

*Don't compromise*

Do everything in your power to do, then stand

*Don't be lazy*

Stand firm

*Don't waiver*

Stand with truth

*Don't lie*

Stand with righteousness

*Don't be immoral*

Stand with peace

*Don't be anxious*

And the grace of God shall guard your heart and mind forever.

My favorite early motherhood moments include watching my daughters try to figure out how to walk. They each walked really well assisted by the walker. That walker would jet and zoom through the house like the walker was on fire with each daughter as the navigator in her time and season. But each one walking by herself was a little different. You could tell they were all a little unsure of their ability to get where they needed to go without assistance. My first two daughters, Rionna and Sarah, caught on to walking fairly fast. By Rionna's first birthday she was walking like she had never moved around any other way. Sarah took until about thirteen months. She tried and fell, tried and fell, but after a while, she tried and walked.

But by the age of fourteen months, my baby daughter Gabrielle was still trying to decide if walking was the way she wanted to move in life. She would hold on to her surroundings and move from one side of the room to the other as long as there was something stable there to hold on to. The true test came when she would get to the end of the couch while trying to make it to a toy across the way. You could see the contemplation on her face—"should I go or should I stay?" "Will I make it?" "What if I fall?" Most times she would drop to the floor and crawl to the toy. Since she was the baby girl, there were plenty of people to get things for her or just pick her up and take her where she needed to go. Why learn to walk? Life for Gabrielle was simple!

We all go through similar things as we are learning to walk with God and in his purpose and design for us. For some women, God calls and they get up and go. For others, trying and falling is the only way to get moving. Then there are those of us who hold on to the seemingly stable things around us asking all the unnecessary questions, "Should I go or should I stay? Will I make it? What if I fall?" Fear of falling keeps most of us from walking in the things of God. It is so much easier to sit and be assisted by others to get where we want to go. It's easier to let our prayer partner or the pastor pray. It's safer to let our husbands preach or run the business. The familiar places and faces around us provide us great comfort as we move through new areas in our lives. We have been deceived into believing that what we feel is more real than what is true. Too many times, what we see and feel is the compromise for the more abundant life we have been promised by God. The best way to ensure that you never reach your destiny is to get too comfortable with where you are and to be too afraid to take a risk. Here is where our faith in God is truly tested.

***"Now faith is the substance of things hoped for and the evidence of things that are not seen." Hebrews 11:1***

If God has called for us to cross to the other side of ourselves, to the side of us that we don't know and can't see, we have to trust that the substance of God knows where He is leading us. Even though we can't feel it, we have to know that the substance of God is much more stable than the world around us. We have to trust that even when there is nothing to hold on to that He will hold us up with His faithfulness and His truth; His love and kindness; His joy and longsuffering. We just have to keep our head up and take it one step at a time.

More than often we can see the prize on the other side. We can see the victory; we can see the place where we have always hoped to be. But the fear that grips our ankles keeps us from letting go. This is where you just have to stand tall with your feet covered in his peace and take the step. And when things around you feel unstable or your faith gets shaken by the cares and the woes, don't go back, just stand. Stand in the assurance that God has not brought you this far to leave you. Stand in the truth that lies within you, that you are more than a conqueror through Christ Jesus and that the work that he has started in you he will complete it until the day of Jesus Christ's return (Philippians 1:6). That itself should be a stabilizing force in your life to balance your thoughts and your concerns—that everything about your womanhood and the process of walking in the high and lifted up places of your emotions, your relationships, your dreams and your desires will continue to be manifested until Jesus comes back. That knowledge should take the pressure of time and its limitations off of you to be or have or achieve this place overnight. Learning to walk takes time and even then we fall sometimes. My baby fell a lot. Sometimes she got back up quickly, other times she laid down in frustration that she didn't get where she was trying to go. But I never saw her quit, and you shouldn't either. Even when she was unsure of how to step or whether she should even try, she got up, balanced herself and just stood still. And she was ok with standing. Her standing still was her time to build her confidence, to determine in herself that she would make a move, eventually.

I pray your time to move is now, but only you can decide. You have been equipped, and you now know your position. Take it, and watch where the Lord will take you. You can wear your heels, now. Walk it out!

# Scriptural Appendix

***Hebrews 12:12-14***

***Therefore strengthen the hands which hang down, and the feeble knees, and make straight paths for your feet, so that what is lame may not be dislocated, but rather be healed. Pursue peace with all people, and holiness, without which no one will see the Lord:***

***Romans 10:15***

***And how shall they preach unless they are sent? As it is written: " How beautiful are the feet of those who preach the gospel of peace, Who bring glad tidings of good things!"***

***1 Corinthians 15:25***

***For He must reign till He has put all enemies under His feet.***

***Romans 16:20***

***And the God of peace will crush Satan under your feet shortly. The grace of our Lord Jesus Christ be with you. Amen***

*<u>John 12:3</u>*
***Then Mary took a pound of very costly oil of spikenard, anointed the feet of Jesus, and wiped His feet with her hair. And the house was filled with the fragrance of the oil.***

*<u>Acts 3:7</u>*
***And he took him by the right hand and lifted him up, and immediately his feet and ankle bones received strength.***

*<u>Habakkuk 3:19</u>*
***The LORD God is my strength; He will make my feet like deer's feet, and He will make me walk on my high hills.***

*<u>Malachi 4:3</u>*
***You shall trample the wicked, For they shall be ashes under the soles of your feet on the day that I do this," Says the LORD of hosts.***

*<u>Matthew 15:30</u>*
***Then great multitudes came to Him, having with them the lame, blind, mute, maimed, and many others; and they laid them down at Jesus' feet, and He healed them.***

*<u>Acts 7:33</u>*
***'Then the LORD said to him, "Take your sandals off your feet, for the place where you stand is holy ground.***

**Psalm 91:13**

***You shall tread upon the lion and the cobra, The young lion and the serpent you shall trample underfoot.***

**Matthew 10:14**

***And whoever will not receive you nor hear your words, when you depart from that house or city, shake off the dust from your feet.***

**1 Thessalonians 2:12**

***that you would walk worthy of God who calls you into His own kingdom and glory.***

**Luke 10:19**

***Behold, I give you the authority to trample on serpents and scorpions, and over all the power of the enemy, and nothing shall by any means hurt you.***

**Proverbs 3:4-6**

***Trust in the LORD with all your heart, And lean not on your own understanding; In all your ways acknowledge Him, and He shall direct[a] your paths***

**Genesis 3:15**

***And I will put enmity between you and the woman, And between your seed and her Seed; He shall bruise your head, And you shall bruise His heel."***

*Psalm 1:1-3*
***Blessed is the [woman] who walks not in the counsel of the ungodly, nor stands in the path of sinner, nor sits in the seat of the scornful, and in His law [she] meditates day and night. [She] shall be like a tree planted by the rivers of water, that bring forth its fruit in its season, whose leave also shall not wither and whatever [she] does shall prosper (female emphasis added)***

*Genesis 35:2*
***And Jacob said to his household and to all who were with him, "Put away the foreign gods that are among you, purify yourselves, and change your garments.***

*Psalm 109:19*
***Let it be to him like the garment which covers him, and for a belt with which he girds himself continually.***

*Isaiah 61:3*
***To console those who mourn in Zion, To give them beauty for ashes, The oil of joy for mourning, The garment of praise for the spirit of heaviness; That they may be called trees of righteousness, The planting of the LORD, that He may be glorified."***

***<u>Proverbs 11:2</u>***
***When pride comes, then comes shame; But with the humble is wisdom.***

***<u>Proverbs 13:10</u>***
***By pride comes nothing but strife, But with the well-advised is wisdom.***

***<u>Proverbs 16:18</u>***
***Pride goes before destruction, And a haughty spirit before a fall.***

***<u>Proverbs 29:23</u>***
***A man's pride will bring him low, But the humble in spirit will retain honor.***

# About the Author

## *Erin M. Anderson*

has been charged by God, with a passion for purpose, to motivate people's minds for success. Erin is an anointed teacher and intercessor, gifted in prophetic dreams and visions. She ministers with power in the areas of prayer, worship and warring for the abundant life promised in John 10:10.

Erin M. Anderson was ordained in 2002 under the leadership of Apostles Michael and Lorelle Rich of Royal Life International Church. Erin has served as an Elder in administration, prophetic counseling, deliverance, and intercession. She is a gifted woman of God in the realm of the church; and she also has been called to the kingdom of education as a leader and mentor. Beginning her career as a counselor in the private school sector, Erin provided individual and group counseling and program design and implementation for high schools. In the public school arena, she served as a Middle School Coordinator for Drug Prevention and Safety and a consultant for parent/teacher organizations. Erin also served as an Assistant Principal in the Metropolitan Nashville Public School System.

Erin holds a B.S. Degree in Psychology, a M.S. Degree in Guidance and Counseling, a M.Ed. in Educational Leadership and is pursuing her doctorate in Leadership and Professional Practice.

Contact Information

Please email:

erinonpurpose@yahoo.com

Or visit:

www.onpurposepublications.com

www.ingramcontent.com/pod-product-compliance
Lightning Source LLC
LaVergne TN
LVHW020651100826
845148LV00012B/2428

*9780982706107*